Afternoon tea
is the ideal way to entertain friends.
A book for tea lovers everywhere.

The
Etiquette
of an
English Tea

Written and compiled
by
Beryl Peters

Copper Beech Publishing

First published in Great Britain by
Copper Beech Publishing Ltd
© Beryl Peters 1995

ISBN
978 1 898617 06 8
1 898617 06 6

A CIP catalogue record for this book is available from the
British Library.

Editor: Jan Barnes
Other acknowledgements: page 62

Copper Beech Publishing Ltd
P O Box 159 East Grinstead
Sussex England RH19 4FS

Thank God for tea!
What would the world do without tea?
- how did it exist? I am glad I was not born
before tea.

Sydney Smith 1771-1845

INTRODUCTION

Sydney Smith's words, uttered so many years ago, are still the sentiments of many present day tea-drinkers. Tea has become an important part of our heritage and its history is fascinating.

Customs and fashions may change, but you don't have to be sitting on an English Chamomile lawn to enjoy an afternoon tea. With the aid of this book, you will be able to recreate a perfect English afternoon tea - wherever you are!

In fact, tea in the traditional English style is riding a wave of popularity around the world and there remains a certain charm about the ritual no matter where it occurs.

Discover why tea became so popular, what effect it had on people, and how society has changed since its introduction.

You will see from some of the verse and sayings what a terrible struggle there was between tea and alcohol! Then you might have a light-hearted dip into the ancient art of reading the leaves or speculate on some of the superstitions surrounding tea.

Try making some of the recipes ..... you'll be able to recreate an afternoon tea for your guests - anywhere - perfectly, knowing that Henry James was a very wise man when he penned the following few words:

"There are few hours in life more agreeable
than the hour dedicated to the ceremony known
as Afternoon Tea."

The tradition of tea drinking dates back to the 17th and 18th centuries and afternoon tea, as we now know it, seems to have been introduced in the early 1800s by the 7th Duchess of Bedford. She needed something to stave off those hunger pangs whilst waiting for her late evening dinners!

She started the vogue of having an afternoon tea sent to her boudoir for herself and her guests. Besides

the selection of teas there was toast "as thin as poppy leaves" and fine breads.

Later, when the afternoon tea began to be served in the drawing room, various sandwiches and pastries were offered to delight the company. It seems that there was always plenty of gossip to accompany the tea ritual too!

Very little changes! Afternoon tea is still an ideal way to entertain friends indoors or outdoors. It offers a chance to meet others and an excuse to indulge oneself, besides slowing down the pace of life for a short time. It remains a splendid custom enjoyed by many.

What could be nicer than whiling away an afternoon at a leisurely pace, surrounded by tempting fare, a bottomless pot of tea and good company?

Beryl Peters

I HOPE YOU'LL AGREE

I HOPE you'll agree
  That a lady at tea
Should never cut cake with a chopper,
  Or throw pieces of coal
  At some pious old soul
Who is wearing her husband's best
  topper ;

Or rub jam on the nose
Of a colonel who blows
That organ of smell like two trumpets,
  Or insist you should drink
  Several cupfuls of ink
And bombard all the pictures with
  crumpets.

"In nothing is the English genius
for domesticity more notably declared than in
the institution of this festival - of afternoon tea.
The mere chink of cups and saucers
tunes the mind to happy repose."

AFTERNOON TEA AT HOME

An afternoon tea offered a reason for women to get together and socialise in by-gone times when their men were busy at business - and women weren't allowed to be!

The mistress of the house would keep the tea caddy locked and spoon it out herself as tea was so expensive and precious. Tea was used with cautious economy for many years.

The middle class ladies soon copied the mode and would spend a considerable part of their income on tea - it was a status symbol!

When the taxes were reduced on tea it became equally popular with the less wealthy and so the tradition of afternoon tea spread.

So, the ladies would send out invitation cards to their friends and acquaintances stating that they would be "At Home" on a particular afternoon. No reply was necessary, but most ladies would turn up unless they had a pressing engagement …. they didn't want to miss the social gossip, and they liked the opportunity to see what everyone else was wearing!

Afternoon tea was always served at five o'clock. The staff would prepare everything according to the mistress's wishes and the servant would bring in the tea tray to add to the pre-set tea table when the lady of the house rang the bell. A good servant would be inconspicuous, but would always be ready with boiling water to refill the pot.

The tea table has hardly changed in two hundred years. The table would be covered with a pretty cloth with matching napkins. There would be a china tea service, teaspoons, a lemon dish and fork, and a vase of flowers. Sandwiches with crusts removed would be served; crumpets which were stored over a bowl of hot water to keep them warm, hot scones, cakes, pastries and sometimes seasonal fruits.

The hostess would always pour the tea, although others could help to offer food around the table, especially the men if any were present. No one would stay after seven o'clock.

The mistress would have instructed the servants in the art of making tea and she would also ensure that her daughters knew the simple rules too.

Tea Superstitions...Should the lid be accidentally left off the tea pot you may expect a stranger bearing ill tidings.

The following method is quoted from *The Afternoon Tea Book* by Agnes Maitland (1915) and still works these days:

"Fill the kettle with fresh cold water, and set it on to boil.

Make the tea directly the water boils.

Never make the tea with water that has been long on the fire simmering, or that has been twice boiled. The natural aeration of the water is drawn off by long-continued heating, and the hardness of the water is increased by evaporation. The more rapidly the water is heated, the better the tea.

Warm the teapot. Put in the tea in the proportion of 1oz to six or seven persons, or a teaspoonful for each person and a teaspoonful over.

Pour on the boiling water. Cover the teapot and allow it to stand from five to seven minutes to draw.

If tea is required in haste, while the water is coming to the boil put the tea into the teapot and stand it inside the oven until it is thoroughly hot through. Pour on the boiling water and in a minute it will be ready to pour out."

Traditional Recipes for Afternoon Tea

Larded Tea Cakes

1lb flour	6oz lard
2oz loaf sugar dust	½ pint milk

Take one pound of flour, six ounces of lard, rub it well into the flour, then add two ounces of loaf sugar dust; mix it in as before, then add the milk, make it into a dough, then roll it out and fold it three or four times, and cut the cakes to the size you would like them.

Lightning Sandwiches, or Five-Minute Cakes

1 teacup flour	1 teacup sugar
2 eggs	2 tablespoons of milk.
1 teaspoon baking powder	

Mix all the ingredients well together, beat the eggs very light, stir them in, add the milk; bake in a buttered tin or on buttered plates.   Split open when cool and spread with jam or lemon cream.

Traditional Recipes for Afternoon Tea

Coffee Buns
(Note: these buns do not contain coffee!)

8oz flour	3oz currants or sultanas
1 tablespoon milk	4oz butter
4oz demerara sugar	1 egg
1 teaspoon baking powder	
Pinch of salt	

Sift the flour, salt and baking powder into a basin, rub in the butter and add the sugar and currants. Beat up the egg, add the milk and mix with the other ingredients to a stiff paste. Put the mixture onto a tin in 12 small heaps and bake in a quick oven for 15 - 20 minutes.

Rations

"Please, ma'am, my ma'am
Sent me to see, ma'am
If you'll come to tea, ma'am,
At half past three, ma'am,
Bring your own sugar, ma'am,
Bring your own tea, ma'am,
And I'll have the kettle boiled
By half past three, ma'am."

1919 Anon

Who wouldn't like to drink afternoon tea
Out in the garden just like me?
With the song of a bird, and the hum of a bee,
And the sun-flowers looking all eyes to see.

The little girl's stirring her tea so sweet;
Tea in the garden is such a treat,
With a cool breeze blowing and not much heat -
And doesn't the tea-tray look
charmingly sweet?

PICNIC TEAS

Although the traditional afternoon tea, served in the drawing room was enormously popular, there were occasions when a less formal setting was sought.

During good weather afternoon tea would often be served outside on the lawn, in the shade of the trees, so that the ladies weren't stifled by the sun's rays or made to perspire! They also needed to protect their delicate complexions.

The tea ceremony was much the same, only removed outdoors where the conversation could revolve around the weather, the flowers and the latest summer fashions.

Tables and chairs would be arranged at the best vantage points and nearby there would be a small table with a spirit heater on which the kettle could be kept at the ready.

The food would be brought out at the last minute for freshness, and fine nets would keep insects off the table. It was all very attractively presented and colour was added by beautifully arranged platters of fruit …. a veritable feast for both eye and stomach!

Less formal picnics offered another outdoor treat and were much appreciated by young couples who found this a good way to spend some time together outside the strict and tiresome confines of the home.

TEA SUPERSTITIONS …To stir the tea in the pot anti-clockwise will stir up trouble.

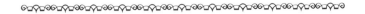

All the family would look forward to a picnic and the food would be planned well ahead and carried in hampers and baskets.

A place by a stream or in a clearing made an excellent spot, with plenty of space for outdoor games for both adults and children.

Many of the picnic places were within easy reach of the home in the early days as most families had to walk. The servants enjoyed the change in routine and would make most of the arrangements, whereas those from a not so wealthy family had to carry everything themselves!

TEA SUPERSTITIONS ...To spill a little tea whilst making it is a lucky omen.

Tea On The Lawn

Come, Celia dear, I've raised the tent,
So let us spread the feast together,
Then take our tea with sunshine blent,
All in the pleasant summer weather.

There you will sit, the hostess dear,
Flashing your smiles above the tray,
And serve our friends with cups of cheer,
While I shall face you - far away!

Those strawberries very tempting look
And grapes, the best of muscatel;
Roses from every garden nook
Arranged as Celia knows so well.

Traditional Recipes for Picnic Teas

Lawn Sandwich

½lb flour   ¼lb sugar
6oz caster sugar   2 eggs
¼lb ground rice   ½ gill milk
1 teaspoonful baking powder
Jam

Sift the flour, ground rice and baking powder together onto a piece of paper, cream the butter and sugar together until they are white, beat in the eggs one at a time and stir in the milk and other ingredients as lightly as possible. Put this mixture into two sandwich tins, lined with buttered paper, and bake in a quick oven for about ten minutes.

Turn them out on to a paper sprinkled with caster sugar. Spread one side with jam, and place the two cakes together.

Traditional Recipes for a Picnic Tea

Ellen's Tea-cakes

1lb flour	2 oz butter
1oz caster sugar	1 teaspoon baking powder
½ pint milk	

Rub the butter into the flour until it is quite fine. Add the sugar and baking powder and mix very thoroughly. Stir in the milk, mixing it to a light dough as quickly as possible. Knead very little. Divide the dough into three; form each piece into a round flat cake. Bake at once in a quick oven; split open and butter whilst hot.

Traditional Recipes for a Picnic Tea

Staffordshire Shortcake

¼lb butter	¼lb caster sugar
2 eggs	4oz almonds
1oz angelica	2oz candied cherries
Flour	

Beat butter to a cream in a basin, add sugar and eggs. Mix together then add blanched and chopped almonds, chopped cherries and sufficient flour to make a fairly stiff dough.

Turn on to a board, roll out to ¼inch thick, cut into squares and diamonds, pinch the edges; bake in a rather quick oven to a pale brown tinge.

Afternoon tea - that pleasant hour
When children are from lessons free,
And gather round their social board
Brimful of mirth and childish glee.

J C Sowerby & H H Emmerson 1880

NURSERY TEA

Five o'clock, and time for tea in the nursery ... but before that the children had to be spruced up and presented to the ladies taking afternoon tea with mother in the drawing room. They only stayed a short while and then at a given signal were hurried away by nanny or the governess to leave the ladies to their gossip! Nanny would give her wards a nursery or a schoolroom tea.

Occasionally "Mamma" would grace the nursery with her presence which would delight both the chil-

dren and the nanny, who might be given an hour's freedom!

It would be a precious time when mother could give her children her undivided attention in a relaxing atmosphere; a special time without social stress; a time when the children could show off their musical and artistic skills and entertain her with some verse. At holiday times father might join the group and play with the children.

The nursery tea would be a more substantial meal than the traditional afternoon tea and would also serve as dinner (except for those rare occasions when the children had to endure the real thing!)

Cook would produce all kinds of treats for the nursery tea especially when there were also visitor's children present. There would be an assortment of neatly cut breads with accompanying savouries, small delicate sandwiches, hot scones or muffins with pre-serves in cold weather, dainty cakes and shaped biscuits.

Traditional Recipes for a Nursery Tea

Nursery Cake

½lb flour   ¼lb demerara sugar
3oz sultanas or raisins   1 egg
1½ oz candied peel   ¼lb butter
1 teaspoon baking powder.
Pinch of salt   ¾ gill milk

Sift the flour, salt and baking powder together in a basin and rub in the butter, add the sugar, fruit and candied peel cut up, and mix well together. Beat up the egg in a small basin, add the milk and stir them into the other ingredients. Put this mixture into a cake tin lined with buttered paper and bake in a moderate oven for about 1½ hours.

Note: Half an ounce of caraway seeds may be used instead of fruit.

This quantity will require a cake tin 5" in diameter.

Traditional Recipes for a Nursery Tea

Princess Cakes

2 eggs plus their weight in butter, sugar and flour
1 teaspoon vanilla essence
3oz glace cherries
1½ oz grated chocolate
½ teaspoon baking powder

Sift the flour, baking powder and chocolate onto a piece of paper. Cream the butter and sugar together until they are white, then beat in the yolks of eggs one at a time. Whisk the whites to a stiff froth, add the flour, baking powder and chocolate and stir in lightly to the butter and sugar. Add the cherries (cut up) and the vanilla essence and put the mixture into small buttered queen cake tins. Bake in a moderately hot oven between 10-15 minutes.

Note: These cakes are good without chocolate too!

Traditional Recipes for a Nursery Tea

Neapolitan Sandwiches

Slices of brown and white bread and butter
Hard boiled egg beaten with mayonnaise
1 basket of cress
Salt and pepper

Spread some of the mixture on to a slice of brown
bread and butter, onto this put a slice of white bread
and butter. Spread some more of the mixture and on
top put a slice of brown bread and butter.

Sprinkle some cress, salt and pepper on this and
cover with a slice of white bread and butter. Press well
together and cut into small rounds with a cutter.

There's money in your tea-pot !

Old-fashioned folk used to keep their savings in the tea-pot. You, too, can get money out of the pot. By using Edglets you can save one spoonful in four.

Edglets tea gives a specially rich infusion, because it is made from the tea leaf under ideal conditions. Edglets is delicate in aroma, full of fine flavour and free from excess tannin.

Ask for

Edglets

Brooke Bonds leaf-edge tea

8 d.

quarter pound.

(Sold only in packets.)

If you cannot readily obtain Brooke Bonds Edglets write to Brooke Bond & Co., Ltd., Goulston Str et, London, E.1. They will see that you are supplied.

Nursery Tea Rhymes

The little girl who used to play
With these same toys, as I to-day,
  Must be so sorry to be dead.
    She cannot spread
The cloth upon the stool with me,
Nor wash the cups, nor make the tea.

They are her tea-things too, and yet
She must lie still and quite forget
  The treasures which she loved so much.
    While I may touch
Her hallow'd cups, or lightly break
All that she prized; she will not wake.

She died a hundred years ago;
How sad that she can never know
  The tea-pot's safe, the cream jug whole,
    I wish her soul
Might come one little hour to play
With these, her toys, as I do to-day.

"Take some more tea," the March Hare said
to Alice, very earnestly.
"I've had nothing yet", Alice replied, in
an offended tone, "So I can't take more."
"You mean you can't take less," said the Hatter:
"It's very easy to take more than nothing."
(Lewis Carroll)

NELLIES VISITORS.

" MAY I offer you some tea ?
Come now, have a cup with me !
Gladly will I welcome you—
Make yourselves at home, now do."

" Thank you, thank you, Mrs. Nell,"
Answered Kate and little Bell ;
" Very pleased we'll be to stay
And take tea with you to-day."

*Tea - a drink which relieves thirst
and dissipates sorrow.*

A CREAM TEA

By the beginning of the 20th century it became fashionable for hotels, department stores and tea shops to serve cream teas.

Tea shops were not something new, they merely became fashionable once again! In fact, the first tea shop in London was opened in 1717!

By the early 1900s there were very exclusive tea shops where one really went to eat the superb confectionery and then 'swill' it down with tea!

Ordinary people did not want, and could not afford, those exclusive tea shops. All they really wanted was a place to sit, with a friendly atmosphere and a good cup of reviving tea - rounded off with a tempting slice of cake or a cream scone.

The manageress of the Aerated Bread Company knew this was what was needed even in 1884 when she persuaded the directors of the A.B.C. to allow her to open a tea shop on London Bridge.

It was an instant success with the ladies because it gave them a place where they could go, unchaperoned, to meet friends and still keep their reputation.

Soon there were tea shops in cities, towns and villages where shoppers and tourists could go to enjoy a cream tea.

People will still make a business rendezvous in hotel tea rooms and many a contract has been discussed over a cup of tea.

TEA SUPERSTITIONS ...Two tea-spoons, accidentally placed together on a saucer, points to a wedding or a pregnancy.

The Savoy of London has been serving afternoon tea for almost all of its 105 year history and to this day there is piano music played at tea time.

At Claridges too, tea is served daily by liveried footmen between three and five o'clock in the afternoon. Indeed, hospitality suites at events like Henley, Wimbledon and Ascot keep up the tradition of afternoon tea, which is often one of the focal points of the day.

It is thought that Garden Parties have been held at Buckingham Palace since 1865 - entrance by special invitation only - and no village fete would be complete without the tea tent! What would we do without a reviving cup of tea?

TEA SUPERSTITIONS ...Bubbles on tea denote kisses.

A Special Cream and Apricot Tea

Fashionable ladies were always trying to outdo their friends and acquaintances when it came to giving afternoon tea. They would devise all kinds of variations, and the cream and apricot tea was one of the most successful.

For this kind of 'cake tea' it is stressed that everything must be very daintily prepared!

The table-cloth should be of fine cream linen, embroidered with apricot silk; a handsome arabesque border above the hem would be a very suitable pattern, which should be repeated in a square or oblong for the centre. Or there could be a border of drawn thread work, sewn with apricot silk. Of course the little serviettes must be worked to match!

Tea serviettes differ from others, as they are only used for laying across the lap. They should be about eight inches wide and eighteen inches long, hemmed neatly at each side, and embroidered and fringed at the ends only.

A well-trained thunbergia plant, with its fragile cream or apricot blossoms, or a begonia of the required shades would look good in the centre of the table!

You may have glasses of cream and apricot flowers lightly arranged with ferns. The tea service should be of cream and apricot china or plain cream.

The tea equipage should be of silver.

Fruit should be served in separate dishes; apricots, white raspberries, bananas with the rind taken off, peeled oranges divided into quarters and covered with sifted sugar, apricot-fleshed melon and any other fruit of the right shade or colour! A rich thick cream should be served.

Bread and butter daintily rolled would be suitable to offer. Small glasses or shells of marmalade or apricot jam placed about the table will give the right tone of colour. Hot scones will suit the colour scheme better than any other tea breads. Shortbread should also be served as it is a nice cream colour!

 TEA SUPERSTITIONS ...To make tea stronger than usual, indicates a new friendship.

Traditional Recipes for a Cream and Apricot Tea

Apricot Cake

6oz butter worked to a cream
Grated rind of half a lemon
6oz white sifted sugar
4 eggs   10oz vienna flour
½oz baking powder   6oz glace apricots

Work butter, lemon rind and sugar until creamy and then add the yolks of four eggs and flour. Stir, then add the whites of eggs, baking powder, and glace apricots cut into pieces. Drop the fruit into the mixture as lightly as possible; put into a lined cake tin and bake for 1¾ hours. When cold, ice the cake with cream coloured icing and ornament with glace apricots cut into leaves and small squares.

TEA SUPERSTITIONS ...If two women should pour from the same pot, one of them will have a baby within the year.

Traditional Recipes for a Cream and Apricot Tea

Savoury Sandwiches

Boil two eggs hard. Shell them and pound them with 2oz butter, salt, a pinch cayenne pepper and a table-spoon of anchovy sauce, which will make the mixture a good shade of apricot!

Cut some bread and butter very thin, spread it with the mixture; lay another piece of bread and butter on top, spread another layer of the mixture on that, and so on, till you have three layers of the mixture.

Then cut the crust off all around, and cut into strips about an inch wide.

It is a little change from the ordinary sandwich!

TEA SUPERSTITIONS …To put milk in your tea before sugar is to cross the path of love, perhaps never to marry.

Hurrah! at length we see it here,
Upon our own tea table placed,
And soon our spirits it will cheer
From out the urn* that it has graced
Let each and all then grateful be
And hail a welcome guest in tea.

* Tea was served from urns in earliest times.

"Let each and all then grateful be
And hail a welcome guest in tea."
Pepys

A remedy for melancholy
is always to keep a tea-kettle
boiling in the hearth.

❦

"A woman is like a tea-bag. It's only when she's in
hot water that you realise how strong she is."
Nancy Reagan

CR∽∿∽∿∽∿∽∿∽∿∽∿∽∿∽∿∽∿∽∿∽∿∽∿

TEA TOWELS

When tea was first introduced to Britain it was served in bowls, following the custom of the Chinese. Later, elaborate tea services were being used and, as the servants were heavy-handed, the mistress herself would take charge of supervising the washing of the china after entertaining. In some cases she would do it herself.

A bowl of water would be brought to her in the parlour or the morning room, along with a small drying cloth. To begin with it was a special piece of linen which was often woven by a local spinster, but hand hemmed by the housemaids as they sat around in their quarters after their main duties were over.

The beautiful Wedgwood and Coalport china warranted this special treatment; it was a prized possession in those early days. The silver mote spoon, devised to capture the small pieces of tea leaves as they came to the surface of the tea, would also need

cleaning each time. Its pointed handle also served to unplug the teapot's spout when it became lodged with big tea-leaves.

Mass-made tea towels were introduced during the Industrial Revolution and their popularity spread by marketing them through the new department stores, which became all the rage. To begin with these "kitchen and glass cloths" had the familiar blue and red band across the centre.

Much later these typical drying cloths gave way to the illustrated versions. Irish linen was considered the best as it was most absorbent and very strong.

The renowned company of Lamont's of Belfast, which had traded since the early 1800s, continued to make the traditional style but also introduced pictorial "tea towels". Since then the tea towel has increased its popularity.

Love and scandal are the best sweeteners of tea.

Matrons who toss the cup and see
The grounds of fate in grounds of tea.

YOUR FORTUNE IN THE TEA LEAVES

The reader refers to the person reading the tea leaves, while *the enquirer* is the person whose cup is being read.

Make a pot of tea, using a small tea leaf, in the usual way. Pour a generous amount into a plain white cup. Don't use a strainer - the more leaves the better.

Now ask the enquirer to sip the tea slowly and make a wish. When about a tablespoon of tea remains in the cup, ask the enquirer to rotate the cup in an anti-clockwise direction three times using his or her left hand before turning the cup upside down onto the saucer.

The handle of the cup should point to the enquirer.
The reader now takes the cup and reads the contents,
by looking for symbols formed by the tea leaves.

The handle represents the enquirer and home. The
opposite side refers to strangers and events away from
home. The rim of the cup is the near future, while the
area close to the bottom shows the distant future. The
leaves form pictures, which is where your imagination
comes in, and intuition helps you to decipher them!

Good luck symbols are: stars, triangles, trees,
flowers, crowns and circles.

Bad luck symbols are: snakes, owls, crosses, cats,
guns and cages.

Now examine the tea leaves for resemblance to
known symbols:-

Anchor	Your love is true to you
Circle	Good luck. If broken, bad luck
Fish	Money
Flowers	Happiness
Heart	A love affair
Horse's Head	Good luck
Horseshoe	Good luck
House	Success
Ladder	Promotion
Mountain	A strenuous climb ahead
Number	Indicative of time - days, weeks, months etc.

Owl	Illness of a friend or relative
Pipe	Trouble
Ring	Marriage
Ship	A journey
Spider	Beware of a cunning enemy
Sword	Complications
Tent	A desire to escape complications
Tree	Good health
Umbrella	Take shelter with your friends
Wheel	Progress
Woman	A happy family

Some say that tea leaf reading involves some kind of clairvoyance, but most believe that the real art of tea-cup divining merely involves understanding the tea-leaf code.

WHAT TEA DOES FOR YOU!

The effect of tea drinking was described by a poet
of the T'ang dynasty:-

"The first cup moistens my lips and throat
The second cup breaks my loneliness
The third cup searches my barren entrails
The fourth cup raises a slight perspiration - all
wrongs in life pass through my pores.
At the fifth cup I am purified; the sixth cup calls
me to the realms of the immortals, and the
seventh cup - ah! but I could take no more!"

Another poet said about tea:-
"It tempers the spirits and harmonises the mind;
dispels lassitude and relieves fatigue;
awakens thought and prevents drowsiness;
lightens and refreshes the body and clears the
perceptive faculties."

೧ೲ♢ೲ೧

We live in stirring times ... tea-stirring times.

TEA THROUGH THE DAY

"I have no favourite tea, but according to the time of day, the mood, weather, the company I am keeping and the food I am eating, so I will select my tea, just as one would with wine.

To start the day, a brisk wake-up tea is English Breakfast; some prefer Ceylon Breakfast which is a gentler way to come to terms with the world!

Lunch time calls for a rounded mellow tea, and Darjeeling is the answer.

In the afternoon the weather governs my choice. On a hot day, with time to spare, to sip Lapsang Souchong with that smoky tangy flavour and nibble a cucumber sandwich or two is very special.

On a warm afternoon, Earl Grey is always refreshing and thirst-quenching, but lemon tea is equally as nice.

On a colder day, try a tea with more body such as Russian Caravan, China Black, or Queen Mary Darjeeling.

On a really foul day one wants cheering up, so then I would choose Assam!

The cocktail hour can also be a time for tea.

TEA THROUGH THE DAY

Blackcurrant, made iced or hot is awfully good with gin, rum or vodka; Ceylon Breakfast, iced, makes an excellent base for a punch.

After dinner, try China teas. To follow a white wine, I like a smooth transfer to China Oolong; after a red wine, Prince of Wales is a fine tea to drink.

To follow a very sticky cloying dessert, Earl Grey comes into its own. It will refresh you wonderfully!

After a heavy meal try Jasmine Tea, the traditional Chinese digestive tea and very low in caffeine.

Finally, after a pleasant evening meal, the tea I have in my own home is Rose, or Rose Pouchong, a light black China tea flavoured with real rose petals. The delicate taste with natural low caffeine is a perfect way to end the day and ensure a good night's sleep."

Sam H G Twining OBE

Give me tea sweet and weak
"Bring me the *Times* and do not speak."
A P Herbert

A Comfortable Cup of Tea

Tea parties meet in friendship and peace,
To young and old they'll never bring disgrace
All drunkards I hope will take an advice from me
Give over drinking whiskey and take a cup of tea.

About Servants

Indeed they're soberly inclined
To another affable and kind;
They never quarrel when at tea they sit;
Tea is the school, at which they learn their wit.
A sober girl's a credit to her sex.
But tippling minx defames 'em when she speaks;
She utters words unseemly to the ear,
That make the hair of honest women flare!
Therefore of all that men and women drink
Tea is the best, pray madam, what do you think?

Answer

It is better than drinking gin by far,
Which makes them stink and causes domestic war.

THE BOSTON TEA PARTY

Taxing tea in the American colonies angered the people to such an extent that they rebelled at the famous Boston Tea Party.

On the 16th December 1773 a group of men, disguised as Indians, boarded ships owned by the East India Company and tipped the cargoes of tea overboard in order to demonstrate to the British government that its rule was no longer accepted.

From having been the favourite American drink, tea became the symbol of oppression and more people started to drink coffee.

"Should I, after tea and cake and ices,
Have the strength to force the moment to its crisis?"
T S Eliot

TEA TATTLE

A heavily used teapot will benefit from an hour-long soak with hot water mixed with a tablespoon of carbonate of soda, to remove stains and residues.

❧

If water has a high mineral content, a longer brewing time may be needed since tea does not infuse easily in hard water.

❧

Tea was first sold from apothecary shops as is reflected by some of the brand names still in existence in Britain today. Typhoo is the Chinese word for doctor: PG Tips stood for Pre-Gestive Tips: 99 Tea was known as doctors' or prescription tea.

❧

The very high taxes on tea in the middle of the eighteenth century led to much smuggling. In 1784 the government was forced to reduce the tax and tea became an affordable drink to all classes.

❧

TEA TATTLE

While tea prices were high, it was common practice for those who were able to afford tea in the first place, to "use the leaves twice, then dry them and pass them to a poorer family".

꧁꧂

Hot water is to remain upon the tea no longer than while you can say the Miserere Psalm [Psalm 51] very leisurely.
Sir Kenelm Digby

꧁꧂

It is alleged that the first command given by Queen Victoria upon her accession to the throne was:
"Bring me a cup of tea and the *Times*."

꧁꧂

A full cup must be carried steadily.

꧁꧂

"I own, that men some gods may over-praise.
But, the worth of tea, no eloquence can raise."

꧁꧂

Acknowledgements:

The author and publishers would like to thank the following for
their assistance in the research for this book.

The Tea Council Information Service
Brooke Bond Ltd
Twinings Tea Ltd
The Savoy Group of Hotels and Restaurants

'Tea Through The Day' reproduced by kind permisson of
Sam Twining. Twinings have been selling tea since 1706
when the Company was started in Devereux Court just off the
London Strand.

Other books in this series:

ETIQUETTE FOR GENTLEMEN
THE ETIQUETTE OF POLITENESS
THE ETIQUETTE OF LOVE AND COURTSHIP
ETIQUETTE FOR CHOCOLATE LOVERS
ETIQUETTE FOR COFFEE LOVERS
ETIQUETTE FOR THE CHILDREN
ETIQUETTE OF DRESS
ETIQUETTE FOR THE CHAUFFEUR
ETIQUETTE OF MOTORING
ETIQUETTE FOR THE TRAVELLER
ETIQUETTE OF NAMING THE BABY
ETIQUETTE FOR THE WELL-DRESSED MAN
ETIQUETTE FOR WINE LOVERS

For your free catalogue containing these and other
Copper Beech Gift Books, write to:

Copper Beech Publishing Ltd
P O Box 159 East Grinstead Sussex England RH19 4FS

Copper Beech Gift Books
are designed and printed
in Great Britain.